Conversations You Need

By Dorian S. Withrow Jr.

ISBN

Paperback: **979-8-9865238-6-6**

Hardback: **979-8-9865238-7-3**

Contact

Website: www.dswjr.com

Email:114realities@gmail.com/

withrowauthors@gmail.com

Table Of Contents

Introduction

Education can come in many forms. Quotes are great ways to get a point across. Quotes allow interpretation; they provoke people to think. They ignite dialogue about many important components to life such as money, relationships, community and family value. It will allow for introspective work and reflection for self development. There are also conversations within this literary work. Each conversation will be centered around the approach to growth and overcoming obstacles. These conversations come from my life. Some, I created around what I learned through schooling. While reading these conversations and quotes, think about how these thoughts can be applied to other lessons and other areas of life. There are a ton of valuable insights on each page. The information is relatable for all ages and any environment.

Family Strengthening

Elder: Hey, how are you doing?

Adwin: I am alright. How are you?

Elder: Are you going to the banquet saturday?

Adwin: I cannot unfortunately, the timing of things is unideal. I cannot take off from work on Saturday night.

Elder: I understand that. I will be going with my eight grandkids and dog. They mentioned that the banquet facilitator said "Well, the dog I do not know, but the kids are allowed in" (followed by a smile and laugh).

Adwin: You have your hands full.

Elder: (nodding) I have my grandchildren often. They are within an arm's reach, all eight of them. On the weekends I have a family dinner. They all come over. I have to clean up after they leave and all, but it is worth it.

Adwin: I like that the grandkids are together often.
That family bond is important.

Elder: My cousins, two boys and two girls, used to
hang out a lot when they were younger. Now that
they are older, people have moved and get busy, but
it is as if things didn't change.
Adwin: I see. (pondering look)

Elder: I like to keep my grand kids together and
have them get along.
Adwin: So they can foster bonds and maintain
family bonds.

Elder: Yes, sir it is great talking to you. I always
enjoy it.
Adwin: Yes sir, so do I.

"The greatest shelter for the ills your children will experience is your words and model."

"Teach your children so they are not misguided by others."

Dorian S. Withrow Jr.

Chances

Adwin: Do you give second chances?

Young Lay: Yes everyone gets a second chance.

Adwin: Really?

Young Lay: Yes

Adwin: Why do you say that?

Young Lay: Everyone gets a second chance.

Adwin: You could be right.

Young Lay: Do you get second chances?

Adwin: (light chuckle) I do.

Young Lay: Do you have second chances?

Adwin: Sometimes, it depends.

Young Lay: Why?

Adwin: Sometimes people don't deserve second chances.

Young Lay: Why do you get second chances?

Adwin: I am still growing and learning, but I make changes so I don't need a second chance again.

Young Lay: Well, people grow and learn all the time, right? So shouldn't everyone get a second chance?
Adwin: (long pause)... I suppose so. I think sometimes people just take more time than others to make changes. (Leans in, whispers) Don't let your emotions blind you.

"If your family and friends can't be wrong, then you have not matured enough."

"Do not make the one a model of the many and do not make the many the model of the one."

Dorian S. Withrow Jr.

Activism

Interviewer Smith: Why did you get into activism?
Adwin: When I see enough trouble, I become bothered by it. I do what I can to alleviate the troubles of others.

Interviewer: Do you think everyone should get involved in activism? There are lots of individuals who may care less or are afraid to step up.
Adwin: Well…When something good or bad happens, no matter the distance, you should get involved. What happens in the community will directly or indirectly affect you. Its effects fall upon representation, economics, and the political climate. The effects influence your family, friends and strangers in some way and therefore yourself. It also affects you and your influence on your family, friends and strangers. Do not live blindly and wait for the problems to be put on your doorstep. Do not wait until your child is haunted by troubles. Do not wait until you experience discriminatory issues at

work. Do not wait until you are unjustly targeted and attacked.

Interviewer: What are some ways people can do activism themselves?

Adwin: One way is sending letters or emails to council members or local politicians. Other ways include addressing your concerns and troubles regarding something in the city, volunteering, or bringing awareness through advertising. The greatest thing we can do is create tools that will combat the problems we face. You should also direct your resources to those tools.

Interviewer: In what ways do you get involved in activism?

Adwin: I get involved in campaigns regarding certain topics such as disciplinary issues in school and economic issues. I display activism in my behavior; carrying a book wherever I go. I also wear clothing with appropriate messages. I shape how people view me and therefore, others alike. I got involved with marches, petitions and so on. More importantly, I teach the younger generation about history and the significance of change while providing practical steps they can take.

Interviewer: Do your books play a part in activism?
Adwin: Yes, but it is not heavily focused upon. I like to give elements of it by addressing concerns and providing something to overcome certain issues.

"Don't make your day any worse by comparing
troubles."

"A determined man can move mountains. An
undetermined man wouldn't move a feather."

Dorian S. Withrow Jr.

Presence

Dr. C: What's up Adwin?! (handshake)

Adwin: I'm doing alright doc. (handshake)

Adwin: Hey, I had a concern, I was in the subway station and the younger fellows were very rowdy and their behavior was disturbing. (chuckle) They are even making fake gangs. None of them could harm a fly. I can't see them heading in the right direction. The cops are even sent every school day. I can't say anything, they'll ignore me.

Dr. C: Look at it like this. You know the environment they came from. A lot of them do not have the proper guidance. Mom and Pop are handling business. One parent might be missing. There are struggles within or outside of the home. The guidance they do have comes from the people on the corner. Am I right?

Adwin: (Nodding) Yes.

Dr.C: The people that need to be in their lives are people like us! Although we are at work, school, and moving around.

Adwin: (Nodding) Mhm.

Dr.C: Get involved in their life. Handle your responsibilities, but volunteer at some youth centers. Engage in local events they might be at. If you can help someone, then do that, but not at your detriment.

"Screaming will open a wound. One's mind may maintain an echo that will keep the wound open."

"There's always a match for a great outcome."

Dorian S. Withrow Jr.

Role model

Jermey: What have you received from your role models or teachers?
Adwin: They helped me think in a very good way.

Jeremy: What do you mean?
Adwin: My great uncle Levi for example, everytime he talked to me, it was about how proud he was.

Jermey: What are some of the things he'd say?
Adwin: Being the first boy out of the great grandchildren, he was happy because he was surrounded by girls all the time. He would say, "Finally!"

Jermey: (Lighthearted chuckle)
Adwin: (bright smile) "Since you were born, I knew you'd be something special. Keep this up; I know you are going to be something great. You are growing up! I used to hold you in my arms, "doe doe. Look at you now, strong. (lil shove) Man, come here" Then he would reach out for a tight hug

rocking back and forth. "Take care of your mother and brother. You are going to do some big things in the world, I can see it. Don't slip up."

Jermey: He spoke love and positivity into you.
Adwin: Most definitely, I didn't appreciate it as much as I do now. From moments like those, I instilled in myself an obligation to conquer.

"I've started saying I could be wrong when people give opposing viewpoints. Even when I am convinced I am right."

"What I once held dear does not appeal to me anymore. At the time it was my prized possession."

Dorian S. Withrow Jr.

Mentor?

Gina: Who is your mentor? Who do you look up to? Who do you go to?

Adwin: (Smile) She made her transition to the ancestors a while ago; my great grandmother. Outside of her, the world is my mentor.

Gina: Why your great grandmother?

Adwin: There is so much to say. (pondering look, downard) She set the foundation for my values, moral and ethical thought. She gave me early discipline. Most of all, it was the way she lived.

Gina: How did she go about it?

Adwin: I got lectured for a long time. Without choice, I'd have to sit or stand and listen to whatever she had to say. There she taught me family values, family history, what to avoid, importance of learning all I can, and the significance of taking care of yourself. She gave that time to help me mentally develop the mind needed for growth.

Gina: The way she lived influenced you?

Adwin: From what I saw she displayed grit. Amongst her struggles, she was a woman who persevered. Regardless of how she appeared to others, she took care of her family. She handled her responsibility; she went above and beyond to juggle the responsibility of others. She stepped in to add balance where my parents lacked some stability.

Gina: I've never heard this before. You say the world is also your mentor.

Adwin: Yes, ma'am. One of the most prominent lessons my grandmother gave me was to "learn from those that came before you." She meant that in the context of family. I remixed it into "Learn from everyone who came before you." No matter who it is, whatever someone did right or wrong should be taken into account. History tells us not only what to avoid, but where to go. When I look at other people, I learn something. I can find something to admire. Something about anyone can guide me. I can not single out anyone to say that is my mentor.

"Success and challenges are siblings born from progress."

"When you find exceptional people, cherish them."

Dorian S. Withrow jr.

Three Lessons

Dom: Have you ever had serious injuries?

Adwin: Yes, I was struck by a vehicle actually.

Dom: Where did you get hit?

Adwin: My right leg and left elbow. (displayed scars)

Dom: Ouch. (disgusted face)

Adwin: Looking back at it, it was a really interesting time.

Dom: How so?

Adwin: After my first surgery, I was laying in bed for a long time. My mother and student nurse suggested I go to the playroom. My twelve year old pride would not allow that. I feared being seen by anyone because I thought being in a cast was embarrassing, weak and incapable. After some convincing, I got into the wheelchair for the playroom. I was stunned when I got there. I witnessed other children with casts, IV's, bald heads and so on. I watched them play and I joined in on the action with the nurse. It took moments to realize amongst the trouble I was having, that I am not alone. I let pride go a little and concluded that my fear was not necessary.

Dom: What was the other lesson?
Adwin: Well, there were several lessons. The second lesson was one that took a mental shift. Shortly after the news about my injury reached my school, I had gotten letters and candy. As a twelve year old, clearly I went for the candy first, judging what I received. (Smile and light chuckle)

Dom: (Light laugh)
Adwin: There's one letter I remember in particular. It was from a teacher and it said "Get well soon, and make sure you look both ways." Many people would take offense to it. They may get angry and seek some kind of retaliation or hold a grudge. I was a little shocked, but I thought about the kind of person the teacher is. I knew the letter was in good

faith. She wanted to cheer me up. On top of that, I am already struggling, so why make it worse.

Dom: Oh I see.
Adwin: She gave some good candy too.

Dom: What kind?
Adwin: Flavored hard candies.

Dom: Was there anything else?
Adwin: Yes. I was home for a long time while healing. The pride thing was still there a bit. I did not want to be seen at school injured. Therefore, I needed a tutor for all of the school work. Looking back, pride kicked me in the behind. I would have been better off going to school. When the tutor came to the house one day, I was complaining about pain in my leg. It really didn't hurt that bad. It was kind of like one of those unnecessary conversation starters. I think I was trying to get out of school work. He told me "I work with people that have disabilities and different kinds of conditions. There

are people who can not move their arms and fingers.
Their fingers are restricted from movement.
Imagine if you could not move your neck at all.
Some can not eat by themselves, wash or use the
bathroom on their own. Although unideal, you are
fortunate to have the few problems you have. The
problems can always be worse."

"Outside of fact, what is right to one is wrong to another and what is wrong to another is right to one."

"There is never a problem if you are blind to it."

Dorian S. Withrow Jr.

Developing Motivation

Young Cam: You do all this stuff; how do you get motivation to move? I do not feel like I am ever motivated.

Adwin: Before I get into my own source, I want to make important points. Target your source of motivation and there are many sources, but here are a few I use. Good students write important information down.

Young Cam: Ok. (gets his notebook)

Adwin: Ask yourself some questions. What will make you proud of yourself? What do you want to accomplish, small or very big? I suggest you keep your sights on the very big things. The small stuff will reinforce probability. What do you do to get yourself in the mental space to do what you have to do?

Young Cam: (Writing)

Adwin: For me, I want to make my family proud. I want to make sure the fruits of their labor are bright and sweet. My goal stems from what I believe my purpose is. My goal is to help people make mental shifts to improve themselves. I want to give people what I learned so that they can make choices that will lead them down a great path. I get myself in the mental space for motivation by holding those things in mind. That's part of why vision boards are important. It keeps your goals and influences close. Look at people doing great in the space you are aiming to become exceptional in. Lastly, make some progress; when you make progress you understand that you are moving forward. That will help you strive to make more progress.

Young Cam: (Worried look) Ok…But-
Adwin: Let me tell you something. We were not born to be mediocre. Be something great and do many amazing things. I believe we all have a mission we were given. Not everyone will be able to discover it. When you do, then you'll have some motivation to keep you going.

"Sometimes it may be good to reduce intellectual boundaries and dogmatism."

"Failed attempts have something good and useful about them. Good attempts have flaws too."

Dorian S. Withrow Jr.

False Guilt

Adwin: Now I'd like for you guys to write down your goal. This thing you've always had your mind on; the thing that you'll be remembered for.

Students: (Thinking and writing)

Adwin: What is your goal?

Young Kayla: I want to become an olympic gymnast.

Adwin: That's awesome, I do not hear that often. And you?

Young Sam: I'll be a part of my father's business and eventually take it over.

Adwin: I see, you have interesting guidance. What's your pursuit?

Young Daniel: (He smiles) I... (hesitates to answer, looks down at his paper, instantly changes his facial expression straight)

Adwin: (Smile) What is your goal?

Young Daniel: I want to write comic books.

Adwin: (Laughs) That's very unique; that is also something I don't hear often. I like it.

Young Daniel: Yes, I want to be greater than the famous comic books writers.

Adwin: (Smile) Listen closely, Be confident in your aspiration. I just watched you doubt yourself. Do not hide and be proud of it. I want to see you meet that goal one day. Look at the people around you. Some like to draw and they might help you network to make things happen. I do not want to see that again, understood.

Young Daniel: (nodding) Yes.

"When I saw the greatness of others around me, I found anything within my mind achievable."

"When others instill the youth with doubt, be the one to help them see the stars."

Dorian S. Withrow Jr.

Jealousy

Moon: Through all that you have done so far, have you come across jealousy?

Adwin: (chuckles) I have; they come in all ages, sizes and statuses.

Moon: How do you handle it?

Adwin: Well, you do not dwell on them. Do not become fixated on someone else or you may become like them.

Moon: Do you listen to what they say?

Adwin: As long as I can hear, I know what they say. I understand where they are coming from when they speak. It is a place of spite towards you and discontentment for themselves. Just walk around with a good heart and do not join them.

Moon: What can we do about these people?

Adwin: Not much, but you can work on yourself and the people around you.

Moon: How?

Adwin: You do not see others as competitors. You look at others as inspiration and motivation. When people win, be happy with them. Encourage others to do the same.

Moon: How do you know if someone is jealous?

Adwin: You listen to what they say. Are they trying to belittle your accomplishments? Do they talk down to you, even jokingly? When you tell them of your accomplishments, are they proud and happy?

Moon: I do not know how to pick things out.

Adwin: Listen to their voice, tone and word choice. Also listen to what they may have said behind your back if you catch wind of it. These people can be to your detriment if you do not distinguish them.

Moon: Yeah, I had trouble with someone. They have a certain aura to them, you know? They are mad at my progress, but I do not understand why.

Adwin: After all, results speak for themselves.

What do you think about it?

"You can not trust one who speaks with two mouths
and looks on with two faces."

"As I grew older, I realized I do not have all the
time in the world."

Dorian S. Withrow Jr.

Locked Potential

Master Ab.: Mr. Adwin, where do you think you
went wrong?

Adwin: I did not slam my heels, I need to spin
harder. (pondering look) I did not catch my kick.

Master Ab.: Yes, (smile) now try again.
Adwin: Yes ma'am.

(Adwin performs some movements)

Master Ab.: Much better, continue to make sure you
are getting more power in your spin. Take notes.
Adwin: Yes ma'am.

Master Ab.: I've noticed something else; you hold
back your power. The strikes should come off
stronger. Do not worry about the right position. Do
not worry about it looking beautiful and perfect. Let
me see the pattern.
Adwin: (nodded his head, thinking face)

Adwin: (performs)

Master Ab.: (while performing) Very good, do you notice the difference? You stumbled and tripped a little, but that was supposed to happen. You put your all into it. There are many times I have fallen and stumbled. Do it often and refine what you are working on. Do not worry about looking silly or making mistakes. Your performance is much better than before.

"Think too much and you'll pause as if you were bitten by a slow loris. Do nothing and you might as well have been bitten by a saw-scaled viper."

"The great teachers know when to let you fall."

Dorian S. Withrow Jr.

Purpose

Bomani: Do you know your purpose?

Adwin: I believe so.

Bomani: What is that?

Adwin: It is to help people. Particularly, to help people make shifts in their mentality to help themselves and therefore others.

Bomani: I think my purpose is to help my family, you know. I want to change the trajectory of my family tree.

Adwin: I see, that is a hefty goal, you can do it.

Bomani: When did you discover yours?

Adwin: There's no particular time I'd say. I noticed when I saw that my words meant something to people. When I witnessed issues around me. What about you?

Bomani: I think when I saw it was possible through others and it's almost instinctual for me.

Adwin: We're on the right track.

Bomani: How do you go about fulfilling your purpose?

Adwin: I use my talent and whatever I take a liking to. Whatever interest I have, I use that also. Taekwondo for instance, I teach people how to defend themselves. The same follows for writing.

"The successful person maintains a vision for the future."

"There are often exceptions, use them to your advantage."

Dorian S. Withrow Jr.

Finding Vulnerability

Diana: Opening up is hard.

Adwin: Why do you say that?

Diana: It is just easier to keep things to myself. I don't need anyone in my business judging me. Besides that, it is not something I learned to do. No one where I come from wants to be vulnerable.

Adwin: I see where you are coming from. Do you think being vulnerable makes you weak?

Diana: Yes, because I do not want to get hurt. People can use it against me.

Adwin: Ok, it might help to think about it like this. Vulnerability will make you strong.

Diana: What do you mean?

Adwin: Well your avoidance of vulnerability comes from fear. That prevents you from releasing all that negative energy, sadness and anger. When you release the bad thoughts and feelings your burden will be lighter. If you do it enough your skin will

strengthen harder than an armadillo. Vulnerability
will also shape a different way of thinking because
you have accepted the trouble and went to war with
it. What used to harm you no longer causes pain or
as much pain.

Diana: How do I get there?
Adwin: Find that person that'll help you bring out
those troubles. This person does not judge you, but
listens very well. This person helps you work
through the internal war. This person will not tell
everyone else your business. They are also someone
that seeks the positive and growth in your troubles.
You can do it.

Diana: Ok. When I get there, I will remember you.
(smile)
Adwin: I can't wait. (smile)

"Your experience is not universal nor is it solely yours."

"I'll take the friend who'd genuinely frown at me rather than a friend who smiles when I'm at fault."

Dorian S. Withrow Jr.

Stick To What You Know

Adwin: How is school doing?

Young Clevon: I got some questions wrong when I raised my hand.

Adwin: What's wrong with that?

Young Clevon: I ended up wrong.

Adwin: At least you tried. I had a similar situation in 10th grade. I was in English class and we had done a writing exercise-

Young Clevon: That's like with me.

Adwin: Yes, (smile) pay attention. I used a certain word I read in a book, paradigm.

Young Clevon: What's wrong with that word?

Adwin: Apparently my use of it. I used it in the context of perception, the way we see things. The teacher at the time told me that's not how it is used.

Young Clevon: Oh, so how were you supposed to use it?

Adwin: Another definition of the same word has to do with patterns. The word is ambiguous, but he did not know that. So after going back and forth a bit, he decided to do an internet search of what the word meant to prove a point. The class got to see the time period of the word and its use, as well as how frequently it was used. He found out that I was right, although a couple hundred years too late. (Chuckle) He followed that up by "Where did you learn the word?" I told him "I read it in a book." He responded, "Stick to the words you know."

Young Clevon: I understand, so what did you do?

Adwin: I used more words I knew that I had obtained the same way I did the word paradigm. Sometimes, we look at people older and/or with education as knowing more, but that's not always the case. Learn and apply what you learned. He intentionally or unintentionally told me to restrict myself. He told me to not expand my vocabulary regardless of what might lead to a mistake. I remind you, I made no mistake. I encourage you to expand and apply. Do not let anyone restrict you.

"Save face by avoiding assumptions; they can be wrong and bring bad thoughts."

"In the presence of adversity, acknowledge that one man can be right in the face of one hundred men."

Dorian S. Withrow Jr.

Overcoming Fear

Dayo: Are you afraid of anything?

Adwin: I am afraid of a lot of things.

Dayo: What are they?

Adwin: Big predators, heights and oceans…

Recently, I went rock climbing.

Dayo: That is something; you are much more brave than me. Doing something like that would make me think you aren't scared of heights.

Adwin: Oh no I was scared, but it was a bit of a journey. It was something new and I wanted to see what it was about.

Dayo: Your fear did not prevent you from climbing? How did you go about it then?

Adwin: Fear did not prevent me to an extent. It's a bit different than being on a rollercoaster where you passively move into fear. I had forced my physical and emotional energy through ambition to reach the top. My ambition was stronger than fear.

Dayo: How did you overcome fear?

Adwin: For me, you have to get over the negative aspects of something that will bring fear. I had to accept that injury and death are possibilities. I'd have to be okay with that happening. Then, you just have to focus on the task at hand. Reassure yourself with some safety measures. We had belts with a pulling system that would prevent me from falling. It is also important to note that you need this kind of "whatever" factor. Anything can happen and I embrace it. The benefit to that kind of experience is that you develop a sense of strength and courage to expand your comfort level.

"Realize the strong are vulnerable; the weak hide themselves."

"Those with something to protect wear a better mask."

Dorian S. Withrow Jr.

Unpleasant Sit Down

Young Zula: How was your day?

Adwin: It was alright.

Young Zula: Just alright? (smile)

Adwin: (Smiles) You know, I never know how to answer that.

Young Zula: Tell me, tell me! (enthusiastically)

Adwin: Well, I took the bus today. There was a woman that decided to sit next to me. There were three seats and we sat on opposite ends. She placed her purse in between us. Within seconds, she gives a frown and retracts her purse clutching it. I see this from the corner of my eye.

Young Zula: What did you do?

Adwin: I did not have an immediate reaction. After some time, I responded "I do not know you either, but your mind is more threatening than I can ever be."

"If someone throws garbage in your fresh spring, do not join them."

"We judge books by their covers, but it is important to read them. You do not know what you've missed."

Dorian S. Withrow Jr.

Complaining

Elder Yaro: You know, I have not heard you complain one time.

Adwin: Good, that means I have made a lot of progress.

Elder Yaro: Progress?

Adwin: I've been riding the wave of growth for a long time.

Elder Yaro: How are you going about that?

Adwin: It doesn't bring much of a benefit to me nor do people care. If they do, for some reason they are either genuine enough to help or seek comfort in knowing you are suffering. There is also a difference between complaining and addressing an issue. Complaints are more about self soothing. Addressing an issue is about taking steps to solve a problem.

Elder Yaro: I get it. You are something else.

Adwin: Besides when you shut your mouth to discomfort, your life seems perfect.

"Complaining brought me and the enemy together.
In the end, I felt worse."

"Complaining is like walking backwards."

Dorian S. Withrow Jr.

Grief

Adwin: What's wrong?

Young Tiwa: (sniffling) My father passed away.

Adwin: I can relate. What do you feel?

Young Tiwa: I am very sad and I miss him dearly.

Adwin: It is not easy. You are doing what you are supposed to do.

Young Tiwa: Really?

Adwin: Of course, get it all out.

Young Tiwa: What did you do when someone died?

Adwin: I bawled my eyes out; eyes red, snot dripping down my face. Big baby!

Young Tiwa: (chuckled)

Adwin: There were some ways of thinking I needed to adjust. For one, I had to get it out. Then I thought about what she left me in the mental sense. She taught me a lot directly and indirectly. After that, I had to accept she was gone in a way, but also it's like she never disappeared. Finally, I reach for the happy thoughts I have.

Young Tiwa: What do you mean she never disappeared? You do not get to see her again. You can't smell her, touch her, or talk to her.

Adwin: That is true. Let me explain. I remember what she looks like. I have pictures of her too. Right now, I can hear her voice in my head. I remember the things she used to say. (chuckle, tears fall.) As you see, this is a process. I'm not as much of a baby as I used to be. (Smile) I also share her blood. In these ways, she lives through me. She didn't go anywhere.

Young Tiwa: (hands over a tissue) So daddy never left?

Adwin: He's closer than you think. You don't carry his blood for no reason. Talk to him often and seek his counsel. Make him proud.

"The more I understood myself and others the more my eyes rained, but the sun shined even brighter."

"We all fill up with bad water from time to time. Release the valves or you'll rot from the inside out."

Dorian S. Withrow Jr.

Alienation

Young Dynasty: Did you have problems while you were in college?

Adwin: (light smile) I had a lot of problems, what do you mean?

Young Dynasty: Like, is there anything you regret?

Adwin: Oh there is plenty, but there is one thing in particular. I alienated myself.

Young Dynasty: What do you mean?

Adwin: Alienated? Think of it like isolation, or being alone.

Young Dynasty: Why is that?

Adwin: I was a bit more occupied with my studies. I was putting my time into martial arts, work and other things on the side.

Young Dynasty: Isn't that what you are supposed to do? Focus on work and studying all that. It is a good thing. Why do you regret it?

Adwin: Yeah that's what we are told. The draw back of that is the decline of precious relationships I could have been forming and maintaining. I was away from people that matter and people I could have been around more before they passed. In the end, it was just a grade. There are things you may not and will not get back.

"Embrace different thinking, but be critical."

"What is most temporary will need more attention."

Dorian S. Withrow Jr.

Understanding The Young

Tanisha: Ariel, hush he is talking. (forces her back into a sitting position)

Adwin: (smile) She's okay-

Tanisha: (slightly embarrassed look) No, no she is being rude. You're taking your time out to teach us about this.

Adwin: When I was young like her, I'd probably be doing the same thing.

Tanisha: I know, but she needs to sit down and listen.

Adwin: Well, there are a lot of other fun things she'd like to do. I get it, I wouldn't want to listen to my boring old self either. I'm not here to tell you how to parent, but I offer a suggestion to be a little more patient with her.

"Sometimes we are so far removed from the past we fight against it."

"Studying history is important, we should take time to study on our own to help those who will come after us."

Dorian S. Withrow Jr.

Being Right

Adwin: What is wrong?

Sisi: I had information about this subject, but people kept telling me I was wrong when I knew I was right.

Adwin: I think we have all run into cases like that.

Sisi: I know, but it was frustrating.

Adwin: It is hard to convince people who are not open minded and shut out from different information especially if it contradicts what they have believed to be true for a long time.

Sisi: How do I deal with it?

Adwin: Let them walk in their ignorance, but also, be accepting that you could be wrong yourself. We can be mistaken.

Sisi: I see.

Adwin: Information changes all the time as well. What we once knew to be true in society can become false later on.

Sisi: Ok, I will carry this with me.

"Do not become dogmatic, it'll make learning harder."

"There is only so much truth you can give. They will batter you over the head with falsehood, especially in numbers. This has been the case for centuries."

Dorian S. Withrow Jr.

Don't Belittle The Bad

Uncle: One thing I've noticed throughout this whole altercation is that you can't beat people down.

Adwin: I know, but I was mad and it just didn't have to be like that.

Uncle: I understand that and maybe I'd be mad too.

Adwin: So what am I supposed to do?

Uncle: Do not bring up what he did wrong. What good will it do for either of you?

Adwin: He needs to know what he has done.

Uncle: I'm sure he is aware. Depending on your tone, expression and how loud you were, it made him feel attacked. He might not have absorbed a word you said.

Adwin: Hm. (pondering look downward)

Uncle: If anything, subconsciously or consciously, you did it to feel better. You bring him down by reminding him of his faults.

Adwin: …

Uncle: Do not belittle him for his wrong doing, but teach him and understand his world. He did not know better and he needed some guidance.

Adwin: Understood.

"Do not make a bad situation worse by trying to make yourself feel better."

"Self reflection can prevent poor communication."

Dorian S. Withrow Jr.

Angry People

Sadik: I had a friend who is dealing with his habits in an unhealthy way.

Adwin: What happened?

Sadik: Yeah, we kinda fell out. I want him to change his ways. It is not leading to good outcomes so I told him what I thought about it. He did not like it and now there is unnecessary tension.

Adwin: Dealing with those kinds of situations is not easy.

Sadik: What can I do?

Adwin: Wait for him to wake up. Think about how you approached the situation.

Sadik: How could I have approached it?

Adwin: You went with your gut. I think you did the right thing.

Sadik: How would you have dealt with it?

Adwin: I am a person who favors honesty and truth. That combination directed at someone can create a mirror for them. When someone is going through troubles, a mirror is sometimes the worst thing to create. They may get angry with you, or say things out of spite. You'll learn how easy it is to become an enemy or just lose a friend. Without honesty and truth, people will not grow. Even worse, what kind of friend would you be if you let them fall and keep falling? Will you help them reach the lowest levels of themselves by neglecting or reinforcing their poor coping mechanisms and reliving the bad consequences they may justifiably experience?

Sadik: Ok, but I may have lost a friend.
Adwin: Hold your head up high. To me at least, you did the right thing. Be easy with your words, tone and actions. Monitor your facial expressions. You didn't let him sink. More importantly, you did not go down with him.

Sadik: Ok, I will try this next time.

Adwin: Hold on, one more piece of advice that'll help. Empty yourself to receive his troubles, but be empty enough to receive his pain as well.. Understand him and use your wisdom from there. We do not always have the answers.

"Honesty can be perceived as a weapon. Innocuous to yourself, yet a danger to someone else."

"Determine what you value in every circumstance. I will not let a friend fall. That is more important to me than my friendship."

Dorian S. Withrow Jr.

Coping Mechanisms

Mashaka: I've been having troubles. There is a lot stressing me out. I do not know what to do. It is like everything is falling apart. What should I do?

Adwin: We were all in this space at some point. One thing for sure, stay away from the detrimental stuff.

Mashaka: What is detrimental?

Adwin: Those things or activities that will worsen your health and derail you from reducing or eliminating the problem. In the end, it will create more problems. I am referring to drinking, smoking, and using others.

Mashaka: What should I do instead?

Adwin: Work on getting rid of your issues.

Mashaka: I understand that, but it will take time.

Adwin: Find things you like to do. Things that will improve yourself mentally and physically. It would be even better if those things also tackled the problems causing stress. Regardless of anything, take care of yourself.

Mashaka: Alright, like what exactly?
Adwin: Is there something you've always wanted to do?

Mashaka: Swimming, tennis and playing the drum.
Adwin: So do those things. Make it cost effective and let it take an appropriate amount of your time. Explore other things you want to indulge. Do things you like to do. Find that person you can lean on as well. The problem will be there, but enjoy yourself. Lastly, how you think about something or someone and how important the thing or person is to you will determine the intensity of your stress.

Mashaka: Asante sana.
Adwin: Karibu.

"The best way to deal with stress is to get rid of the cause."

"Fight your problems head on. If you neglect them, they may win the war."

Dorian S. Withrow Jr.

To Forgive

Lonan: Do you forgive people?

Adwin: I do, but there are cases where it will take a bit of processing.

Young Lonan: How do you forgive?

Adwin: It's subjective. I do not think there is something universal about it. It is about what you fill your head with. Then, the intensity of the offense against you is another factor. When you can understand those two ideas then I believe you are off to a good starting point.

Young Lonan: What should I fill my head with?

Adwin: Fill yourself with the things that will help you perceive situations and people in a neutral light. Don't see that person as neither bad nor good. That part can be hard sometimes. (chuckle) You could also shape your mind to see things as a benefit in some way. What are some ways of thinking about the offense to help you negate your negative thoughts?

Young Lonan: I do not think that will work for everything?

Adwin: That's completely up to you and how intent you are on forgiving. Also remember, I said intensity matters. We do not know what is unforgivable or forgivable until we experience something that will push us to either side so we take it as it comes. Try not to be consumed by the wrong doing.

Young Lonan: How do I get to the point where I can forgive most things at least?

Adwin: Prepare yourself; fill yourself up with the knowledge that will enable you to endure and overcome an offense. It can be religion, reflection of your experiences or philosophy.

Young Lonan: So I learn that stuff?

Adwin: That's part of it. If you get anything out of this conversation remember forgiveness does not mean laying down and accepting the offense. It does not mean the offense is acceptable in any way.

Forgiveness is about potentially amending the relationship and allowing you to think in a much more healthy way and live happier. You have then eliminated or at least reduced the burden.

"Your backpack of burden always feels better when it is light."

"Forgiveness is not only for you, but for everyone around you. You affect others through your baggage."

Dorian S. Withrow Jr.

Role Models & Mentors

Young Qani: You spoke about role models before.
What kind of role model should I get?
Adwin: That's sort of a subjective question. I can
not tell you who to look up to and learn from.

Young Qani: What do you mean?
Adwin: Well, what do you think you need from this
role model?

Young Qani: I think I just need someone to help me
get over my fears and help me to become much
more outspoken.
Adwin: So find someone who has a history of the
same thing or something similar to your experience.

Young Qani: They can relate to me? (whisper,
thinking face)
Adwin: Exactly. They would be better able to suit
your needs. There are some other things to consider.

Young Qani: What is that?

Adwin: Look at their position in life as well as their shortcomings. I am a person who believes there is something admirable in everyone. Just think about what position or status you'd like to be. Is that person in that place or near it?

Young Qani: Oh yeah. So if I want to be a businessman or something like that I should be around someone who is doing business.
Adwin: Mhm. There are detrimental behaviors people do to themselves or others. You need to be wary of their emotional and habitual faults; poor character, drugs, alcohol and more, you know things along those lines. I say this because I value a clean body and a long lasting one.

Young Qani: Ok.
Adwin: The last thing is you have to judge their emotional states. Is he or she generally angry or miserable? Are they devious towards others? Do they hold jealousy and spit on others?
Young Qani: I think I understand now.

Adwin: We all have some things to work on. Understand them, but take whatever useful information you can get. Do not let their shortcomings bleed into you.

"Make sure the people you look up to are not moving down."

"Let your role model be the example you aspire to reach and beyond."

Dorian S. Withrow Jr.

Time

Young Oluyomi: Hi Adwin!

Adwin: Oh there you are! How is home?

Young Oluyomi: My parents are alright and my siblings are getting into some trouble.

Adwin: Same old, huh?

Young Oluyomi: Unfortunately.

Adwin: It is good you are not leading them that way nor are you following. I know you put some jewels in their ear. Be patient with them, some people just need a little push. Talk some sense into them in a compassionate way. What did you do today?

Young Oluyomi: Thank you, but I did not do much. I watched tv and played a game for some time.

Adwin: Anything productive?

Young Oluyomi: (shameful expression, shook her head no)

Adwin: I'll admit I used to do the same thing, but even less nowadays. I'm not upset with you. I advise you to use your time much more wisely. You are just a little younger than me. I'm a bit content with what I have done with my younger years. I heard often from the older folks that they have regrets about what they wish they could have done.

Young Oluyomi: I do not know what else to do?
Adwin: What have you always wanted to do? Create something, produce something, or learn something unique. Discover and use your talents. You have a lot of free time. How old are you?

Young Oluyomi: I am seventeen.
Adwin: (enthusiastically) Alright, how long ago was fourteen?

Young Oluyomi: Three years ago. (light chuckle) It doesn't seem that long ago.
Adwin: Exactly, I was twenty, two years ago and I feel like it was last week. You have time, but not all

the time in the world. As long as you live you will consistently sculpt yourself. Don't let your greatness go to waste.

"While young and flexible, bend and flex in many directions."

"There is no time limit on growth, except when you waste your own time."

Dorian S. Withrow jr.

Resolving Arguments

Nasha: How do you deal with arguments?

Adwin: I've learned in my studies not to for certain reasons. I do my best to avoid it if I suspect it is coming.

Nasha: Why avoid arguing?

Adwin: Well, there is not much of a positive resolution on either side unless people are mature, open and understanding. Some people seek to triumph over one another.

Nasha: I do not try to bring anyone down.

Adwin: That is very good, although others do not hold the same thoughts. They think they are in battle. Your words will be twisted and manipulated. They will add or delete any of your words to suit their needs. Not only that, they may be unwilling to change their mind if it suits them. They can be too dogmatic in their thoughts.

Nasha: I do not know what to do?

Adwin: Say what you have to say and leave it alone.
If you feel like more needs to be said, then do not
venture far. Let them carry on as they are. You
know what you know and that might be enough.
Save it for someone else.

Nasha: Even with friends and family?
Adwin: It depends, but be willing to lose them in
the process. I want unity in our relationships.

"When immature and unlearned, a battle of words
will almost always make an enemy."

"Arguments can be the fire that burns a bridge."

Dorian S. Withrow Jr.

Criticism

Miyanda: Have you ever been criticized?

Adwin: Yes, I have.

Miyanda: How do you deal with it?

Adwin: It's how you think about it. We are all a bit different in terms of handling criticism based on our history. Intensities of criticism vary and so on.

Miyanda: How should I think about it?

Adwin: First understand where people come from in terms of your relationship and what you know of them. They could be trying to tear you down or bring you up. Their approach may appear harmful, but it could be in good faith. Most importantly, look in the mirror. We have our faults whether we are aware of it or not. At times, it is a matter of perspective for either side.

Miyanda: Oh...

Adwin: Mhm, so keep that in mind, but be aware your good family and friends want what is good for you. Take it in a positive and constructive way. If the criticism is destructive, then teach them otherwise. If they are unteachable then ignore criticism and continue to develop yourself.

"Others' words can form a mirror we may not like."

"While they dissect you, examine those pieces."

Dorian S. Withrow Jr.

Changing My Mind

Jawara: You seem to change your mind on things a lot. You do not hold the same ideas often.
Adwin: That is true and it works for me.

Jawara: Why do you do that?
Adwin: When I get a hold of information that contradicts what I believe or hold true, I put it into question. As I think it through, I change my mind or I don't. I know that I can be wrong in ways.

Jawara: I see, you do not think the same.
Adwin: Yes indeed, I do not look with the same eyes. I am better for it because I get rid of any negative ways of thinking or unproductive thoughts.

Jawara: How do I do it?
Adwin: You have to learn and take on different ways of thinking. Listen and watch with an open mind.

"You do not necessarily have to move with the masses, but you must move."

"Like a snake we need to shed, shed our minds."

Dorian S. Withrow Jr.

Self Discipline

Young Jenue: Do you have troubles? The things that you struggle with, like guilty pleasures.

Adwin: I most certainly do. I have one guilty pleasure I am ashamed of in particular.

Young Jenue: (Eyes wide open, then a curious look.) What is it?

Adwin: You don't believe I have my struggles? (laugh) I love candy, it is not a good thing to eat. It may taste good, but overall it is a nuisance.

Young Jenue: A little bit can't hurt here and there.

Adwin: Many people think that. Do not follow that thought. Candy will weaken your body and harm your teeth. It will raise your sugar to unhealthy levels bringing health risks at your doorstep. You have to be a lot more responsible to your body.

Young Jenue: I mean it can't be that bad if you have a little?

Adwin: It can; then we can consider money you won't get back. Not only do you lose, but you get no return. My guilty pleasure gradually took away from something more important that I could use the money for. It took away from my future physically and financially. A little can add up and self discipline can prevent a ton of issues.

Jenue: I get it now.

Adwin: Take care of your body. You come in with it, but you do not leave with it. It's the only thing we have while living and sometimes we do not treat it as good as we should. Avoid what can harm you.

"Self reflection and self interrogation are your best
friends."

"Control over yourself can prevent a lot of
hardship."

Dorian S. Withrow Jr.

Gratitude

Keldon: I am very stressed. I have a lot to worry about, especially the stuff I do not have right now.
Adwin: What are you going to do about it?

Keldon: (fearful expression) I can not even think right now. I am so thrown off.
Adwin: You have so much to be appreciative of. If you take more account of that from time to time, then it may ease your mind.

Keldon: What do you mean by that?
Adwin: What are you grateful for or appreciative of?

Keldon: That doesn't mean anything to me, Adwin. I am having trouble.
Adwin: (shrug shoulders) You have access to food at will. You have more than enough clothing to keep you comfortable. You can shower as you please. You even have a climate controlled vehicle.

Keldon: (Looks downward with shame)

Adwin: You have a lot more to be happy about than to be stressed over. The problems are real; you need to learn and stay active to overcome them. Focus on the sunshine through the storm sometimes.

Keldon: I am sorry about getting worked up.

Adwin: You are human, there is nothing to be sorry about.

"You are influenced by what you are focused on."

"You have so much to be happy for. I call it
sunshine. Do not take it away just because you see
clouds forming or even rain."

Dorian S. Withrow Jr.

Using Others

Chaga: Some people are so mean. I watched some kids at school use someone else to get what they wanted. The person being used has a good heart and I believe he just wanted to fit in or wanted to genuinely help.

Adwin: Yeah, I assure you that does not stop at their age. (chuckles) It is not a good thing and it also creates issues for relationships.

Chaga: I wanted to say something, but I did not know what to do?

Adwin: It is best if people learn about other individual's inherent value.

Chaga: Like what?

Adwin: Philosophy is a good start. People that use others have ill intentions. It shows selfishness and they may form relationships around such a thing. Those relationships do not last long. They may also experience a lot of mistrust towards others based on their own behavior. We see others in relation to what we do.

Chaga: I mean we need people to help us with things.

Adwin: We all have wants and needs that others can help us fulfill, but do not make usefulness the priority. Make and maintain a connection to someone for who they are, not what they provide.

"If you see people through the eyes of usefulness, they become a tool to you, disposable."

"If a connection with anyone is based on use, relationships are shallow and short. "

Dorian S. Withrow Jr.

Perseverance

Adric: I like your talk about perseverance. I saw an advertisement for a pill that will relieve an issue. I think it is good. They advertised it like it would resolve it without having to do anything.

Adwin: (smile) I take morning classes for ITF Taekwondo. We go through our warm up exercises and then we stretch. Some of the stretches are tough. Depending on your physical condition, it can be easy or difficult. Some people struggle holding the stretch. As we are stretching, my grandmaster would say "Make sure you breathe, you can not buy this feeling at any store." He acknowledged that one of the lower ranks had a lower stretch than he used to on his splits. When he started, he could barely touch the ground with his hands.

Adric: He sounds like an interesting man. (laugh)

Adwin: There's this natural inclination we have to making things easy for ourselves. I think most of us would prefer the easy way, even though there are drawbacks.

Adric: Why do you say that?

Adwin: There isn't much of a journey and it leads to a lack of appreciation for the process. What follows is that the problem may come back. People may revert back to things that brought them the problem. I acknowledge that there are a variety of conditions that bring about unfavorable results.

Adric: You think people taking the hard road will make us better?

Adwin: Not necessarily. I think adversity is a necessity for maintaining progress after we hit the finish line.

Adric: What if adversity is not enough?

Adwin: I take a little bit of this from my grandmaster. Little achievements go a long way. If you are making progress, acknowledge it and embrace it. Then you'll know that you are moving as opposed to being stagnant. I believe that setting goals brings you growth. Making achievable and realistic goals tracked by both you and an accountability partner can also go a long way.

Adric: You have an accountability partner?
Adwin: I did, I need to find a new one. (Smile) I met him in college and he was a cool guy. I went to this man for acknowledgement of my achievements and disappointments. I spoke honestly to him... most of the time. (chuckle) When I needed criticism and scolding, he was the man to go to. He kept me in line when I was off of it. He gave praise when I brought back something worthy.

"It is ok to pick up small stones; it is ok if it took a little longer to search. Stack them."

"Turn discouragement into motivation. If you stop, you'll feel something worse than disappointment."

Dorian S. Withrow Jr.

Smile

Dayo: You don't smile much. (thinking face) You do not have to be so serious all the time.
Adwin: I'm not serious, I am just neutral and calm. There is not much to be serious about.

Dayo: Oh, well I guess so.
Adwin: Don't assume my emotional state is solely based on facial expression. The same relaxed face you called serious would be interpreted as anger if an anger inducing situation arises. This applies to nervousness too, but one thing people do not say is I am happy when I have a relaxed face. They always assume I have an uncomfortable emotion.

Dayo: It is hard to read your face so I do not know what you are feeling.
Adwin: Then ask me, do not assume. There is also a flip side to this. There are people who exclaim words that are contradictory to their face; the one who gives a fake smile and disappointing tones.

Those are the people often under turmoil. Those people wear their expressions bravely.

"Learn the real smile and you may distinguish a friend."

"Avoid assumptions, you can judge wrong."

Dorian S. Withrow Jr.

Uncertainty

Ebele: (Thinking) What are you ordering?

Adwin: I think I will try that. (Puts his finger on the food item)

Ebele: (Shocking look and curiously) Have you had that before?

Adwin: No, but I'd like to try something new.

Ebele: You will spend money on that? It will take time for it to come and it is not like you can return it. You won't know if you'll like it or not.

Adwin: I could get the usual, but I want to expand the amount of food items I like.

Ebele: (He gave a "You will see kind of look") I do not know.

Adwin: (Laughs) You make the same choices out of fear and comfortability. You do not know what else you may like unless you explore. You will remain stagnant and rigid in your choices. If it is good, then

I have succeeded. If I do not like the food, I'll finish it and then I will know what to avoid next time.

"The one who rejoices in your failed attempt, they receive satisfaction. Understand, they failed themselves at that moment. They have sunken even lower."

"Do not let uncertainty imprison you."

Dorian S. Withrow Jr.

About The Author

Dorian Scott Withrow Jr. was born on April 13th, 2000, in Buffalo, New York. His education was primarily through the Amherst Central School District. Dorian began his blossoming in high school by facing and conquering many challenges. His achievements were within many programs he was involved in; programs such as Youth of the Year, Jack and Jill of America, Leadership Buffalo, and Breaking Barriers. He was accepted into Canisius College in 2018 and majored in Animal Behavior Ecology and Conservation (ABEC), with a minor in Philosophy. Throughout college, Dorian was still involved in Breaking Barriers attending meetings, participating in activism, and doing podcasts. He was also involved in his newly found passion, ITF Taekwondo. Dorian graduated from Canisius College in May 2022.

Youth of the Year (Boys and Girls Club)

Youth of the Year is an achievement that youth in Boys and Girls Clubs accomplish for community involvement, leadership, character, and even mentorship for younger people. People who receive this honor not only receive recognition, but have the opportunity to move on to greater milestones. Youth members selected from different Boys and Girls Clubs around the city are offered to take part in different workshops to meet the next stage. These workshops include public speaking, writing, teaching, etc. He did not meet the next stage, but out of six competitors, he came in second.

Jack & Jill Of America

Dorian was also involved in Jack & Jill of America, a program for young black males. The program held many workshops such as leadership, fitness, dress to impress, public speaking, and dance (West African and Urban Ballroom). This program allowed for the creation of a network among its members. Community service was another element of the program to instill the importance of serving exposure to many unique people and aided Dorian in character development. At the end of the program, boys become men through African rights of passage. The final ceremony involved our speeches, dance, and rights of passage. The boys got to give themselves a name when they became men. Dorian became Adwin (thinker and artist).

Leadership Buffalo

Leadership Buffalo was a program Dorian experienced during his first retreat. He met a lot of interesting people from special backgrounds. Leadership Buffalo also held a lot of workshops regarding leadership, cooking, dining etiquette (lesson from a former butler of the queen of England), diversity, inclusion, and more. There was an amazing opportunity for teamwork and building more connections.

Honors and Rewards

Dorian received many honors and rewards in high school. Dorian obtained the national honors society for maintaining merit roll in high school. He also attended Harkness Erie One Boces for Animal Science and earned the national technical honor society. Dorian gained scholarships from Buffalo Urban League and Delta Sigma Theta Sorority. Finally, he graduated from high school in 2018 and pursued a bachelor's at Canisius College. Currently, he is a Canisius alumnus with a Bachelor of Science. Dorian had a strong liking for philosophy. His love for philosophy has led him to earn a place in Phi Sigma Tau, a philosophical honor society, and be rewarded with the St. Thomas Aquinas Award in Philosophy for having demonstrated exceptional achievement in philosophy. Lastly, he was granted the Martin Luther King Award for promoting social justice, social harmony. civil rights, human rights, advocacy of the poor, and non-violence.

Dorian is a graduate and still a youth council member of Breaking Barriers, a program in which males of color ages twelve to twenty-four, act on policy, mentoring, leadership, and improving work opportunities and conditions of other young people in education (just to name a few). Dorian gained very valuable knowledge and developed many meaningful connections. Dorian has had the opportunity to become a social justice trainer and continues to engage in the Breaking Barriers podcasts.

ITF Taekwondo

Dorian is also a martial artist and ITF Taekwondo practitioner. He has some knowledge of Isshin Ryu karate from his grandfather. Dorian started ITF Taekwondo in May 2019. Through diligent and persistent work, he achieved a master's club affiliation. He also takes part in D.E.L.T.A. (Dedicated, Enthusiastic, Loyal, Teaching, Assistant) Team where he can assist in teaching and uplifting others' lives. Dorian is officially an Il-Dan and passionate about further training.

Thoughts Of Creativity King 114 Realities

Thoughts Of Creativity King 114 Realities is a creative self-help book. It is composed of unique free verse poetry, illustrations, haikus, and short stories. The purpose of this book is to help people cultivate themselves and think about their existence. The goal is to inspire people to make changes within themselves and others around them. Through free verse poetry, readers contemplate concepts of forgiveness, vulnerability, social issues, and goals. Illustrations bring an authentic and sincere visual aspect to the poetic work. Haikus add flavor of small implementation of imagery and meaning. The author also added short stories. These are personal stories from his life. These stories have moral and ethical lessons to help people overcome their troubles and misconceptions about life. This book took six years to produce. The work in this book comes heavily from experience. The experience comes from his own life and his perception of other people's condition, action, and mentality. Readers will learn from him and themselves by contemplating the literature and analyzing their reflection on their own life. This book allows people, young and old to read something relatable. The creative components will develop the reader's cravings for more. One goal for this book is to put it in the hands of the youth within schools nationwide. It will act as a supplement to poetry and storytelling in English classes. The book will ignite students' thinking about what kinds of topics can be discussed in the classroom. It will help students in developing their poetry. The beauty of poetry and storytelling within the classroom is that it assists in self-expression. In a sense, this book can be a tool to use as and develop coping mechanisms. When students are struggling with their emotions or expressing themselves, they can revert to this book, as a result, improving their emotional and mental well-being. This book is also suitable for creative writing programs, classes, and workshops. Dorian is

working on his third book that will supersede the
last books and all expectations.

THOUGHTS OF
Creativity
KING
114 REALITIES

Dorian Scott Withrow Jr.

Wisdom 45 Advice

    Wisdom 45 Advice is a book composed of 45 different topics that touch on important subjects such as friendship, communication, vulnerability, money and more. The topics are filled with life lessons and philosophy.

Withrow LLC

Withrow LLC is a consulting company for helping people become authors. Its mission is to help people meet their aspirations. Other services include speaking engagements and healing circles. Speaking engagements touch on topics of self development, growth and goal setting. Healing circles allow people to partake in a comfortable, confidential and welcoming space for vulnerability, overcoming, growing and bonding.

Books Authored By Dorian S.Withrow Jr.

Book Alphabetical

Speak! Young Brown People, Speak. We are listening!
A.L. Savvy Publications 2014, 2022

Thoughts Of Creativity King 114 Realities. Dorian
Withrow Jr., Withrow LLC, Buffalo NY, 2022

Wisdom 45 Advice. Dorian S. Withrow Jr., Withrow
LLC, Buffalo NY, 2022